SHOW ME HOW
I Can Have a Party

Easy decorations, food and games, shown step by step

THOMASINA SMITH

ARMADILLO

This edition is published by Armadillo,
an imprint of Anness Publishing Ltd

www.armadillobooks.co.uk; www.annesspublishing.com;
Twitter: @Anness_Books

If you like the images in this book and would like to investigate
using them for publishing, promotions or advertising, please visit
our website www.practicalpictures.com for more information.

Publisher: Joanna Lorenz
Project Editors: Sophie Warne and Richard McGinlay
Photographer: John Freeman
Designer: Edward Kinsey
Production Controller: Stephanie Moe

ACKNOWLEDGEMENTS
The publishers would like to thank the following children, and their
parents: Aimee, Brooke, Catherine, Chloe, Christopher, Clive, Daniel,
Deborah, Houw, Jason, Moriam, Nicholas and Patrice.

PUBLISHER'S NOTE
The level of adult supervision needed will depend on the age and
ability of the children following the projects. However, we advise that
adult supervision is always vital when the project calls for the use of
sharp knives or other utensils. Always keep potentially harmful tools
well out of the reach of young children.
Although the advice and information in this book are believed to be
accurate and true at the time of going to press, neither the authors nor
the publisher can accept any legal responsibility or liability for any
errors or omissions that may have been made nor for any inaccuracies
nor for any loss, harm or injury that comes about from following
instructions or advice in this book.

Manufacturer: Anness Publishing Ltd, 108 Great Russell Street,
London WC1B 3NA, England
For Product Tracking go to: www.annesspublishing.com/tracking
Batch: 1419-23415-1127

Contents

Introduction

This book is full of great ideas for making your party extra special. The step-by-step projects cover all the ingredients of a good party: games, decorations, food and costumes.

Some of the projects here follow a theme. If you are excited by a particular theme, maybe you could make everything for your party follow the same idea. Some of the themes included in this book are Christmas, desert island, funfair, Easter and Halloween.

You can have as much fun preparing for a party as during it.

Treasure chests are good for hiding presents in.

When Making Things:

1 Try to leave yourself plenty of time before the party.
2 Read through the instructions carefully.
3 Make a list of all the materials and tools you will need. You may need the help of someone older than you. This could be for finding or buying materials or tools.
4 Prepare your work space. Cover the surface you are working on, in case you spill anything. Make sure you have enough room.
5 Put on a smock or apron to protect your clothes, or wear old clothes that are already stained.
6 When cooking, wash your hands thoroughly.
7 Always clean up as you go along. Make sure anything that might spill is in a safe place.
8 At the end of a project thoroughly wash brushes in lukewarm water with a little detergent. Put lids on paints. Wipe surfaces.
9 Be extra careful with sharp tools, scissors or knives. Always make sure the tool is pointing down, away from your face. If you are unsure, ask someone older for help.
10 If you're not sure what to do, always ask a grown-up for help.

Protect your clothes if you are going to do something messy.

Cover your work surface with newspaper or plastic.

Crocodile tunnels are fun to crawl through.

Handy Techniques for Doing Things

In this book there are some handy tips for doing things which can be a bit difficult.

Cutting a Circle Using Scissors

It's very easy to end up with a jagged edge. The best method is to draw your circle then cut into the middle of the circle first. Cut lines from the middle to the edge, so that the circle is divided into segments. Only then do you cut away at the edge of the circle. By cutting the segments you have allowed more freedom for the scissors to move around.

You can decorate a cake to match the theme of your party.

If you need to use scissors or a knife, ask an adult for help.

Painting Round Objects

It helps when painting an object, especially when it's curved, like an egg or a ball, to rest it in a holder. That way it won't roll around when it is drying. Plastic pots, mugs and egg cartons make excellent holders.

A mixture of glue and water can be painted over the surface of paint. This makes it waterproof and protects it as well. It is see-through when it has dried.

Painting Straight Lines

If you find painting a straight line difficult, use masking tape. Stick the masking tape on first. Paint your line and leave it to dry. When you remove the masking tape – carefully – the line will be straight and even.

Round objects are easier to paint when they are propped up.

Masking tape helps you to paint a straight line.

Templates and Guides

Some of the projects in this book have pattern templates for you to draw. There are also guides for some other projects showing you the correct measurements to follow.

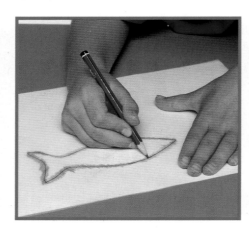

1 Place a piece of tracing paper over the template pattern in the book. Holding the paper still, trace the pattern using a soft pencil. Turn the tracing paper over and scribble over the outline with your pencil.

2 Turn the tracing paper over again and place it on your sheet of paper or cardboard. Draw around the outline of the pattern, pressing hard with your pencil. It will transfer onto the paper or cardboard.

3 Remove the tracing paper and make sure the line has been transferred. Go over the line with a pencil if you need to. Cut out the template and then draw around it as shown in the project pictures.

Dinosaur template

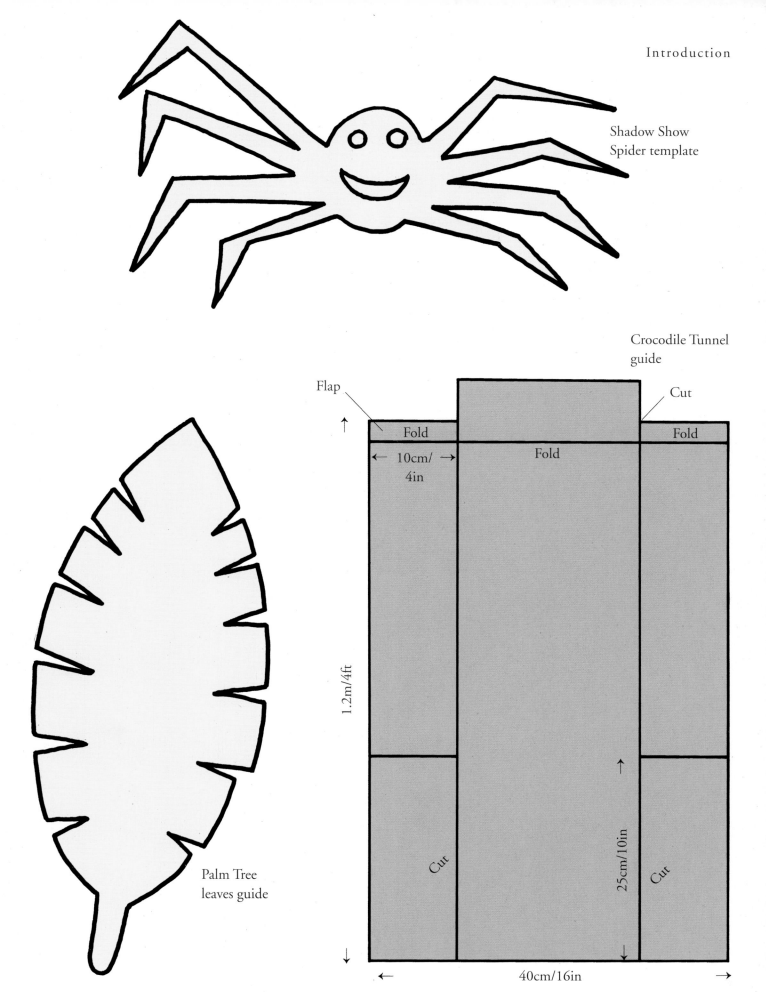

Shadow Show
Spider template

Crocodile Tunnel
guide

Palm Tree
leaves guide

Materials and Equipment

There are some basic tools and pieces of equipment that are used again and again in this book. A ruler, a pencil, scissors, paintbrushes and a glue brush are all essentials.

Most projects involve a fair amount of sticking. The white glue used in the book is known by several other names, such as PVA glue and wood glue. This glue takes time to dry, but once dry it is very strong. When sticking flat paper onto a flat surface, white glue can make wrinkles and lumps, so for that sort of job it is better to use a glue stick. Remember that glue sticks dry up very quickly if you leave the lid off. Masking tape is good for holding things together while they are drying.

Paint

Paint is also known by different names. The paint used in this book is acrylic paint, which is also called poster paint.

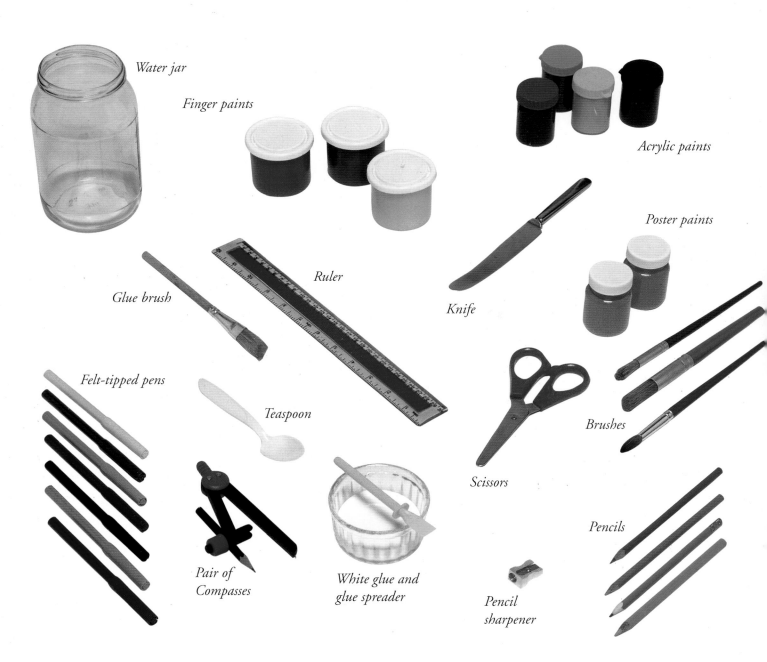

Water jar

Finger paints

Acrylic paints

Poster paints

Glue brush

Ruler

Knife

Felt-tipped pens

Teaspoon

Brushes

Scissors

Pair of Compasses

White glue and glue spreader

Pencil sharpener

Pencils

If you need to paint a large surface, such as the crocodile tunnel, it is worth using emulsion (or latex) paint which you can buy in 0.5-litre/1-pint and 1-litre/1-quart cans. All these paints are water-based. This means you have to wash your brushes and hands in water to clean them afterwards. But you have to wash the paint off straight away, before it dries.

You can get hold of a lot of the materials in this book for free. Cardboard boxes are great to use as strong cardboard. Try to save a few after food shopping. Egg cartons are fantastic.

Here we only have one mask made from an egg carton, but they are also used to hold things while you paint them. Yogurt pots are also very useful, not only for making things but as holders for keeping things still while painting.

Finally, whatever you are doing, look after your materials and equipment. Keep your tools in a box. And lay out any papers flat so that they don't get crumpled.

Have a great party!

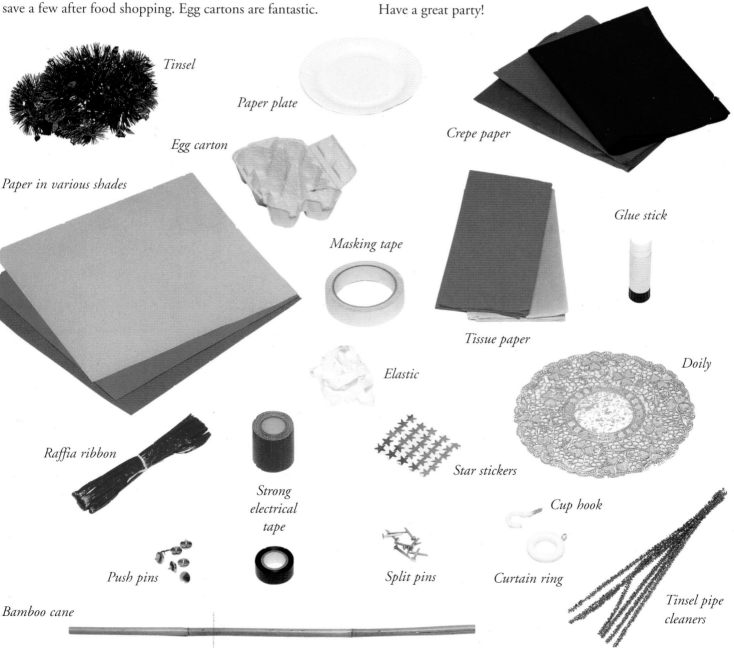

Tinsel

Paper plate

Egg carton

Crepe paper

Paper in various shades

Glue stick

Masking tape

Tissue paper

Elastic

Doily

Raffia ribbon

Strong electrical tape

Star stickers

Cup hook

Push pins

Split pins

Curtain ring

Bamboo cane

Tinsel pipe cleaners

Paper Chains

Paper chains are a must for every party. They are fun and easy to make. You can decorate your home by hanging them along walls and over doorways and they look great with balloons. You may need to hang them up with push pins, so make sure you ask a grown-up first. Aimee is making some special, patterned paper chains. Use as many bright shades as you want to. At Christmas use festive, seasonal green and red.

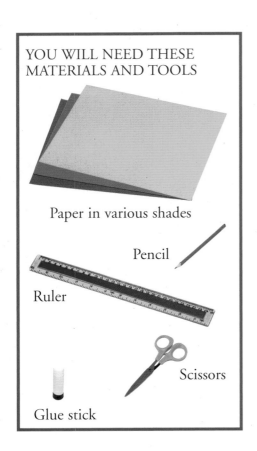

YOU WILL NEED THESE MATERIALS AND TOOLS

Paper in various shades

Pencil

Ruler

Scissors

Glue stick

1 Using a pencil, draw lines lengthways down the sheets of paper. Draw the lines a ruler's width apart – about 4cm/1½in.

2 Draw a line across the paper, so that each rectangle on the paper measures 25cm/10in.

3 Cut out the rectangles as carefully as possible. Aimee is cutting several sheets of paper together, to save time.

4 Make two piles of rectangles, with the same number in each pile. Fold all the rectangles in one pile in half. Draw a lattice pattern on them.

5 Cut out the pattern on all the rectangles in the pile. Keep the paper folded while you cut. Make sure the cuts are even.

6 Unfold your cut-out rectangle and stick it onto a plain rectangle from the other pile. Stick it on using a glue stick. Repeat this until you have made all the rectangles into the links for your paper chain.

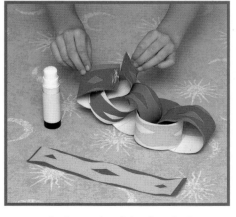

7 Stick the ends of the first link together. Put another link through the first one and stick the ends together. Repeat this with all your links.

You can make plain links, too, to mix and match.

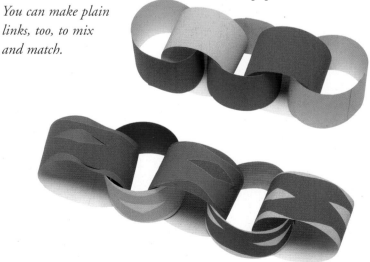

Palm Trees

Treasure Island parties are great for having adventures. You can dress up as pirates and sailors. Nicholas is making some palm trees to put on the table with all the party food. An adult could help you to make larger palm trees, to stick in the yard or around the driveway. All you need to do is make them with larger sheets of paper or stick several sheets of paper together.

Where to put it
Put your palm trees in places where they won't easily get knocked over!

YOU WILL NEED THESE MATERIALS AND TOOLS

2 pieces of thin cardboard, or thick paper: one orange and one green

Tracing paper

Soft pencil

Scissors

Adhesive tape

3 wooden barbecue sticks

Sand

Yogurt pot

Green electrical tape

Kitchen foil

Yellow electrical tape

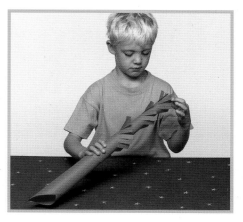

1 Draw a 40cm/16in x 20cm/8in leaf on green cardboard. Use the guide to help you. Fold the leaf in half and cut it out. Make three for each tree.

2 Roll the orange cardboard into a long tube. Hold the tube firmly, so that it doesn't uncurl, and cut a fringe into the top edge of the roll.

3 Still holding the tube firmly, gently pull out the inside edge of the cardboard. Pull it right out to make the trunk of your tree.

4 Use adhesive tape to hold the trunk together at the base. Trim the base, so that the trunk can stand up straight.

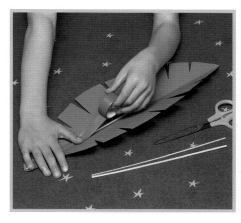

5 Tape a barbecue stick down the middle of each palm leaf with green tape.

6 Snip two slits on opposite sides of the trunk, just big enough to take the stalk of the leaf. Make the slits 10cm/4in from the top of the trunk.

7 Slide a palm leaf into each slit. Push the third leaf into the top of the trunk and tape it in place.

8 Cover the yogurt pot with foil. Stick stripes on it with yellow tape. Fill the pot with sand and push the palm tree into it.

"I Am Four" Badge

Deborah is making a badge to show everyone how old she will be at her birthday party. Make one for your age and wear it with your best party outfit. You could also start a collection for every birthday. Age badges make great presents, too! The badge is made from papier mâché, which is paper soaked in glue mixed with water.

Crafty collecting tip
Cardboard boxes are always handy to have around for making things. If you don't have any bright paper, use pages from a magazine instead. Some of the pictures are great for making flowers. Make sure you ask, before you cut up someone's magazine!

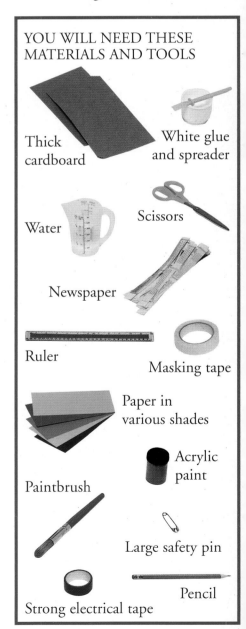

YOU WILL NEED THESE MATERIALS AND TOOLS

Thick cardboard

White glue and spreader

Water

Scissors

Newspaper

Ruler

Masking tape

Paper in various shades

Acrylic paint

Paintbrush

Large safety pin

Strong electrical tape

Pencil

16

1 Draw your chosen number on cardboard. Cut it out carefully and draw around it onto three more pieces of cardboard. Cut out the numbers so that you have four cardboard numbers.

2 Prepare the papier mâché by mixing equal amounts of white glue and water in a bowl. Cut newspaper into strips, and leave them to soak in the glue and water.

3 Meanwhile, stick the four cardboard numbers together with glue. Then stick masking tape round them to hold them together.

4 Paint the badge with glue using the brush, and stick on a layer of wet paper strips. Leave to dry in a warm place and then stick on a second layer.

5 While the papier mâché is drying, cut out paper flowers from bright paper. Cut out circles for the middles of the flowers.

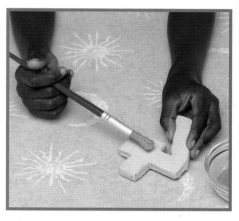

6 Paint your badge with acrylic paint. You might need to use two layers of paint to cover the newspaper. Leave to dry.

7 Glue on the paper flowers, then glue on contrasting circles for the middles. Leave to dry.

8 Use strong electrical tape to stick the non-opening side of the safety pin to the back of the badge.

Birthday Present T-shirt

Why not make this T-shirt as a birthday gift for a friend? They could wear it to their own party! It is important that the painted ribbon is identical to the real ribbon. To achieve this, you may have to mix fabric paints together to make the right shades.

As a special treat you could use green, red and gold to paint a Christmas version of the Birthday Present T-shirt. In place of the spotty green ribbon, use a glittery gold ribbon. The dots on the T-shirt could become bunches of holly.

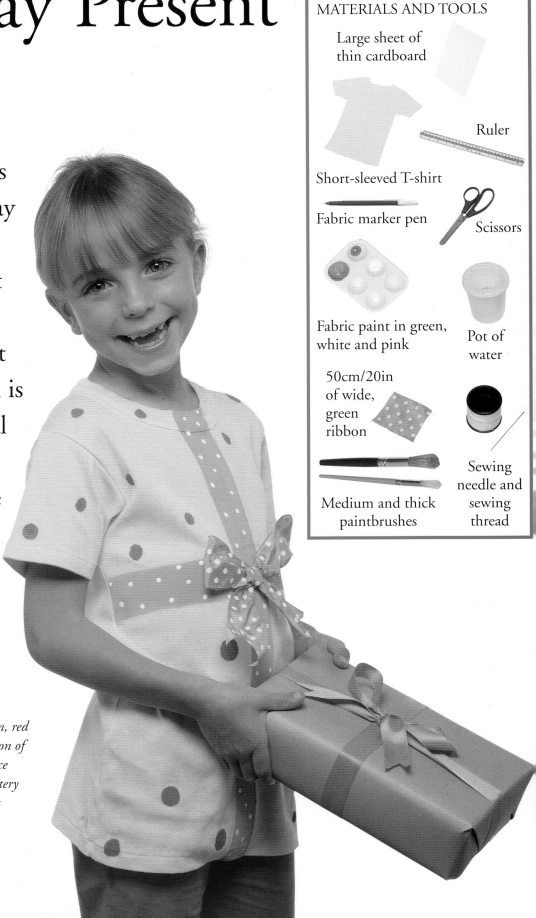

YOU WILL NEED THESE MATERIALS AND TOOLS

Large sheet of thin cardboard

Ruler

Short-sleeved T-shirt

Fabric marker pen

Scissors

Fabric paint in green, white and pink

Pot of water

50cm/20in of wide, green ribbon

Medium and thick paintbrushes

Sewing needle and sewing thread

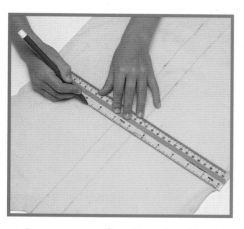

1 Insert pieces of cardboard inside the body and sleeves of the T-shirt. Use the ruler and fabric marker pen to draw two parallel lines down the middle of the T-shirt and two parallel lines across the T-shirt.

2 Paint the area inside the lines with green fabric paint. Do this with the thick brush. These are the pretend ribbons on the present. Make the edges of the ribbon as straight as possible. Allow to dry.

3 Use the medium brush to decorate the painted ribbon with small dots of white fabric paint. Wash and dry the brush before using pink fabric paint to cover the rest of the T-shirt with larger pink dots. Allow to dry.

4 Cut a neat V-shape from both ends of the ribbon.

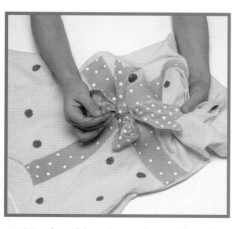

5 Tie the ribbon into a bow. Thread the needle and tie a knot in the end. Position the bow where the painted ribbons cross and sew it into place.

Making fabric paint go further

When you are painting large areas with fabric paint, it is a good idea to add a little water to the fabric paint. This will make your fabric paints last longer and make them easier to apply. It will also make the paint slightly lighter and it may take longer to dry. The more water you add, the lighter the paint will become. Do not make the fabric paint too runny or it will drip all over the place.

Tropical Bird Mask and Wings

It's really simple and fun to make fancy dress costumes, whatever the theme. Brooke has made a fantastic tropical bird, with wings and a beak. She is going to wear it to her Easter Parade party. Make sure the paper you use is quite thick so that it doesn't tear if you run around.

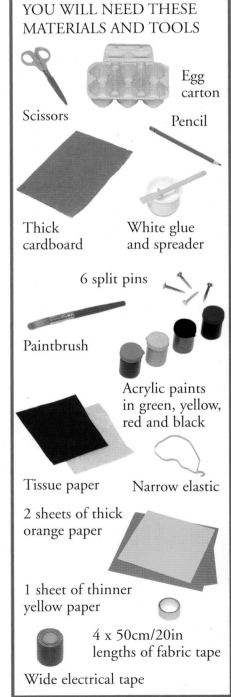

YOU WILL NEED THESE MATERIALS AND TOOLS

Scissors

Egg carton

Pencil

Thick cardboard

White glue and spreader

6 split pins

Paintbrush

Acrylic paints in green, yellow, red and black

Tissue paper

Narrow elastic

2 sheets of thick orange paper

1 sheet of thinner yellow paper

4 x 50cm/20in lengths of fabric tape

Wide electrical tape

Helpful hint

It is easier if a friend or grown-up helps you fit the elastic on your mask, so that it isn't too tight or too loose. Ask an adult to pierce a hole in each side of the mask with scissors or a skewer.

1 Ask a grown-up to help you cut the eyes and beak from the egg carton. Cut two egg compartments with the spike between them. Cut eyeholes.

2 Cut out big eyelashes from the cardboard. Fold and glue the ends to the eyes. Push split pins through both layers and open out. Leave to dry.

3 Using acrylic paint, paint the eyes green, the eyelashes yellow and the beak red. Add a black line around the eyes and the beak. Leave to dry.

4 Cut feather shapes from tissue paper and glue onto the eyelashes. Ask an adult to make holes in the sides of the mask. Thread the holes with elastic, so that it fits around your head.

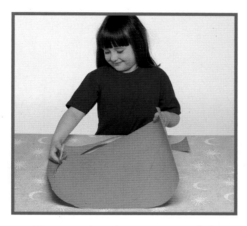

5 Draw a wing shape on one of the sheets of orange paper. Make the wing as big as possible. Cut it out and draw around it onto the second orange sheet. Cut out the second wing.

6 Roll up the piece of yellow paper and cut it into curly, feather-shaped strips. Stick these onto the orange wings with glue.

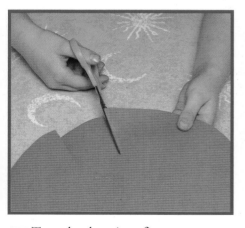

7 To make the wings fit onto your shoulders, make three cuts about 8cm/3in deep, at the top of the wings.

8 Overlap the paper cuts and fasten with a split pin. Use the tapes to tie around the upper arm and waist.

21

Wicked Witch Mask

Make yourself a hideous witch disguise to wear to a Halloween fancy dress party. To complete your transformation, make a broomstick from twigs and branches and wear a black cloak over your shoulders.

Handy hint
If you cannot find a plastic funnel to use for the witch's nose, form a cone from a piece of thin cardboard. To make a cone, cut out a circle 15cm/6in wide. Cut the circle in half. Bend one half so that the straight edges overlap. Join the edges with tape. Trace around the base of cone onto the plate. Draw a slightly smaller circle inside the outline. Cut out the small circle. Make short snips up into the base of the cone. Fold out these flaps and push the cone into the hole. Glue the flaps to the back of the plate.

YOU WILL NEED THESE MATERIALS AND TOOLS

Pencil

Plastic funnel

Paper in various shades

Scissors

String

White glue and brush

Black felt-tip pen

Acrylic paint and brush

Elastic

Raffia

Paper plate

Electrical tape

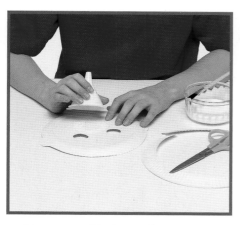

1 Draw a witch's face with a pointy chin onto the back of a paper plate and cut it out. Cut out holes for eyes. Place the funnel in the middle of the plate and trace around it. Cut out the circle, slightly inside the drawn line. Glue the funnel over the hole.

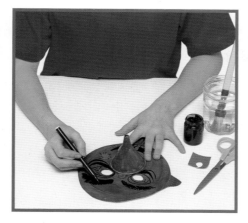

2 Mix a little white glue into green paint – the glue will help the paint stick to the funnel. Paint the face and funnel green. Cut out a small circle of red paper and glue it to one cheek to make a wart. Draw on other features with a black felt-tip pen.

3 Undo the bundle of raffia and cut it into long lengths for the witch's hair. Tie the lengths of raffia together at one end with a piece of string. Use a piece of electrical tape to fix the bundle of raffia to the back of the plate.

4 Make a hole on each side of the mask. Thread a long length of elastic through one hole and tie it on. Put the mask on your face. Cut the elastic to the right length and knot it onto the other hole.

If this gruesome green mask does not scare your friends and family, then nothing will. To really play the part of a witch, make up some spooky spells and carry around a pot full of plastic spiders and frogs!

23

Christmas Tree Hat

Nicholas has made a special hat to celebrate Christmas. It has a star of Bethlehem on top, just like those you find on Christmas trees. He will definitely be the star of the party. You can make other hats, too, such as a sunshine hat or a flower hat for a summer party. Make the hat in the same way but with a big sun or flower instead of a star.

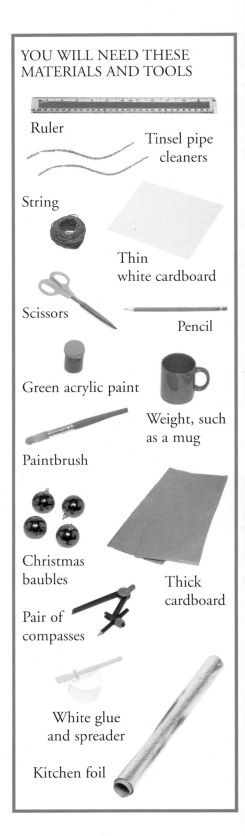

YOU WILL NEED THESE MATERIALS AND TOOLS

Ruler

Tinsel pipe cleaners

String

Thin white cardboard

Scissors

Pencil

Green acrylic paint

Weight, such as a mug

Paintbrush

Christmas baubles

Thick cardboard

Pair of compasses

White glue and spreader

Kitchen foil

1 Measure your head with the piece of string, then add 8cm/3in onto the length of the string.

2 Cut a piece of white cardboard the same length as the string. Draw a dotted line down the middle. Draw a Christmas tree with tabs top and sides.

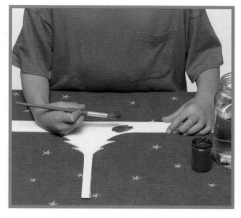

3 Cut out the tree shape with the tabs at the top and sides. Paint it green and leave it to dry.

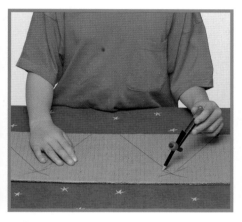

4 On a piece of thick cardboard, draw and cut out two triangles with 18cm/7in sides. Draw the bottom of the triangle first, then use the compasses to mark the top point.

5 Stick the two triangles together to make a star with six points. Glue foil onto the star and leave it to dry.

6 Glue the tab at the top of the tree to the back of the star. Leave it to dry under a weight, so the two pieces bond strongly together. Ask a grown-up to trim the tabs to fit.

7 Glue or tape the side tabs together, so the hat fits your head. Leave to dry. Tape tinsel around the hat.

8 Use tinsel pipe cleaners to tie Christmas baubles around the hat.

Treasure Chest

Aimee has made a treasure chest and she has filled it with prizes, so that each of her guests leaves the party with a going-away present. She has wrapped all the presents in gold paper, so that they look like treasure, and added bags of chocolate coins. The presents don't need to be big or expensive, just fun. She is going to hide her treasure trove until the end of the party, then everyone will play "hunt the treasure chest". The winner gets the first pick of the prizes.

Safety tip

When making holes with a pair of scissors, always make sure the blades are closed together and that you point the tip of them away from you.

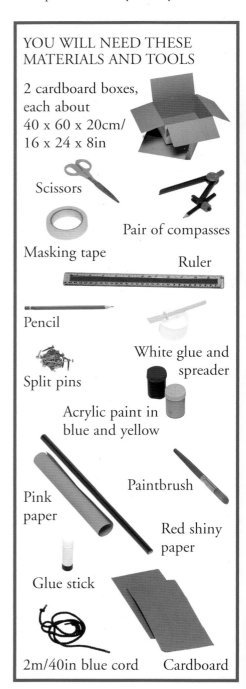

YOU WILL NEED THESE MATERIALS AND TOOLS

2 cardboard boxes, each about 40 x 60 x 20cm/ 16 x 24 x 8in

Scissors

Pair of compasses

Masking tape

Ruler

Pencil

White glue and spreader

Split pins

Acrylic paint in blue and yellow

Pink paper

Paintbrush

Red shiny paper

Glue stick

2m/40in blue cord

Cardboard

1 Cut three of the flaps off one of the boxes, leaving one of the long flaps. This will be used later for the lid.

2 Cut up the second box, leaving the base, one long and two short sides. Draw a semicircle on each short side.

3 Use the compass to draw the semicircles, as shown in the picture for Step 2. Cut them out.

4 Fold up the semicircles to make the sides of the lid. Place the long side of the box in the middle and hold in place with masking tape.

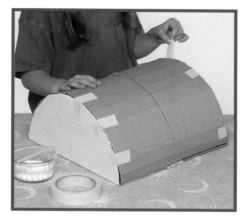

5 Cut a 60cm/24in square of cardboard. Ask a grown-up to score the cardboard to help it bend. Glue it to the sides and secure with tape.

6 Cut the flap on the first box to make two hinges. Glue the lid onto the hinges and leave to dry. Stud with split pins, putting glue under each pin.

7 Paint the outside of the chest with blue acrylic paint. With the glue stick, stick on yellow stripes to create a barrel effect. Add a keyhole and pink skulls and crossbones.

8 Line the chest with paper. Pierce two holes in either side of the box base. Thread cord into each and knot, then glue onto the lid. Hold in place with masking tape until dry.

Crocodile Tunnel

Moriam has collected lots of big cardboard boxes to make a fantastic crocodile tunnel. She has made it so that her friends can open and close the mouth, as the crocodile eats them up! If you like, make another animal instead: an elephant, a horse or a big snake. Another great idea is to make just the crocodile's head. Put up a tent in the garden and use the head for the entrance. You can crawl inside and sit inside your fat crocodile's stomach!

YOU WILL NEED THESE MATERIALS AND TOOLS

Big cardboard boxes that will fit around you

Cardboard

Ruler

Scissors

White glue and brush

Pen

Masking tape

Split pins

Pair of compasses

2 paper or plastic cups

1 litre/1 quart green emulsion (latex) paint

5cm/2in paintbrush

Acrylic paint: black, red and white

Medium paintbrush

1m/40in string

1 Cut the two short top flaps of a cardboard box into triangles. Cut the two long flaps to have a straight edge 30cm/12in long. Open up the bottom.

2 To make the snout, cut out cardboard 40cm x 1.2m/16 x 48in. Use the guide to help you. Cut zigzags for teeth, and flaps as marked.

3 Cut up to the lines, and glue the corners together. Secure them with split pins. Repeat for the other half of the croc's jaw.

4 Attach the snout to one long flap of the box you prepared in Step 1. Use glue, masking tape and split pins.

5 Cut out two pieces of cardboard 15 x 10cm/6 x 4in. Use compasses to make a curve on each and cut out.

6 Draw around the cups. Cut out two circles with scissors, and fit the cups into the holes.

7 Attach the eyes onto the top of the head by folding the straight edge and gluing it down. Hold each eye in place at the top with a split pin.

8 Paint your crocodile head. Ask a grown-up to pierce a hole in the nose. Thread string through and tie a knot at each end. This will allow you to open and close the mouth.

For the croc's body, open up other cardboard boxes, glue the flaps and paint. Now prepare to be gobbled up by the hungry crocodile – chomp!

Shadow Show Spider

Halloween is the celebration of spirits, spiders and witches. Nicholas is making some shadow sticks to cast larger-than-life shadows. You can make a whole spooky shadow show. Hang up a white sheet and stand behind the sheet with a light behind you, or stand in front of a light and cast shadows onto the walls. You could make other shadow show shapes – the more witches, bats and toads the better!

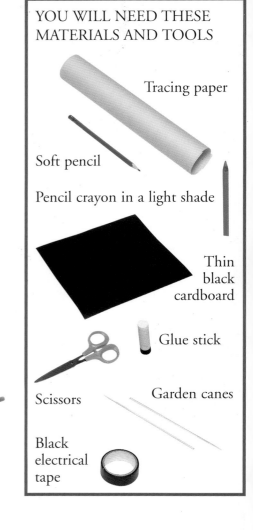

YOU WILL NEED THESE MATERIALS AND TOOLS

Tracing paper

Soft pencil

Pencil crayon in a light shade

Thin black cardboard

Glue stick

Scissors

Garden canes

Black electrical tape

1 Copy the spider template onto tracing paper. Scribble over the spider in light pencil crayon.

2 Turn it over, then draw around the outline with an ordinary pencil to transfer the spider onto the cardboard.

3 Cut out your spider around the outline of the template. Be careful not to cut the legs off!

4 Cut out little strips of cardboard to make the spider's fangs. Glue them into place, using a glue stick.

5 Tape the garden cane onto the back of the spider with black electrical tape. Hide the cane behind one of the spider's fangs.

You could also copy this sinister shadow witch, or make up your own scary shapes.

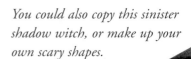

Arty Party Wall

Making a fun wall is always a huge success at parties. Party goers can draw on it, and leave messages or their names. Here Christopher has drawn a picture of the sea, but you can choose any theme. Leave lots of crayons and pencils in jars next to the wall. You'll be left with a masterpiece.

Material brainwave
If you can't get hold of a large roll of paper, you could buy some lining paper or simple patterned wallpaper from a decorating store.

YOU WILL NEED THESE
MATERIALS AND TOOLS

Several sheets of paper in various shades

Scissors

Pencils in various shades

Glue stick

1 large roll of paper, approximately 1m/40in square

Push pins

Balloons

Black electrical tape

1 Cut out long wiggly strips of green paper to make seaweed.

2 Draw the outlines of some fish on sheets of paper, using light pencils on dark paper. The fish should be quite large. Cut them out neatly.

3 Cut out eyes and patterns from another shade of paper and stick them onto your fish with a glue stick.

4 Pin or tape your large sheet of paper to the wall. Decorate the corners with balloons. Ask a grown-up to help if you are using pins.

5 Stick on your cut-out fish and seaweed. Arrange them so that they look nice, but leave room for other drawings, too.

6 At your party, draw on lots of other creatures with your friends. You could write messages and add streamers to the decorations, too.

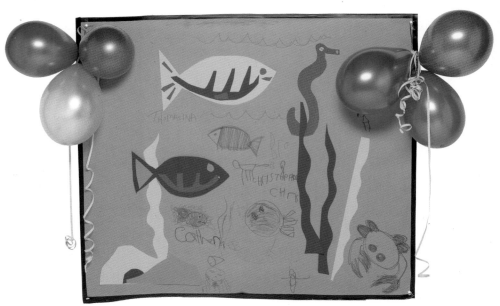

Gone Fishing

Houw is making a fishing game. Each player has to hook up as many floating fish as possible when the music is on. The player who catches the most fish wins. This game is best played in the backyard or kitchen, as it's easy to splash lots of water around. Houw has used large plastic bowls to make his fish ponds, but paddling pools are great as well.

Material note

The number of rods and bottles will depend on how many friends want to play. Make sure there are about three fish bottles per player.

YOU WILL NEED THESE
MATERIALS AND TOOLS

10–20 small plastic drinks bottles with screw tops

Paintbrush

Acrylic paint

String

White glue and spreader

10–12 curtain rings

5 bamboo canes

Scissors

Blue food dye

Electrical tape

5 plastic-coated screw-in cup hooks

Tissue paper

2 or 3 large plastic bowls

1 Wash the drinks bottles and soak off the labels. Leave to dry, then screw the lids back on. Paint fish shapes onto the bottles. Mix glue into your paint so that it sticks to the plastic.

2 Cut string into lengths of 45cm/ 18in. Tie the end of each piece of string onto the hook in a curtain ring. Do this with as many curtain rings as there are bottles.

3 Tie the string onto the bottles with a double knot, so that the curtain ring dangles a bit.

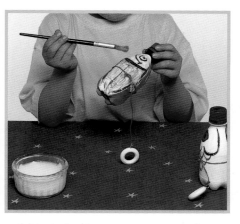

4 To make the paint waterproof, mix a varnish of three parts glue to one part water. Apply two coats to the painted fish bottles. Leave the glue to dry between coats.

5 To make the fishing rods, decorate the bamboo sticks with bands of electrical tape.

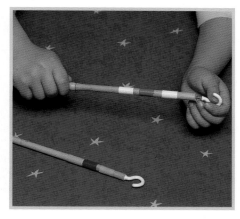

6 Screw a cup hook firmly into the end of each rod.

7 Wrap tissue around the bowls. Add food dye to the water.

35

Coconut Shy

You don't need coconuts to make a coconut shy. Gaby is making her own version of the game you find in funfairs. Her game has lots of funny faces. To play, set your coconut shy on a table. Make sure there is space behind and in front. Mark a line in front where the players have to stand. Then try and knock the faces out of the pots with the little ball. Make sure the pots are weighted down and tied to the table. Have as many as you need – eight is a good number.

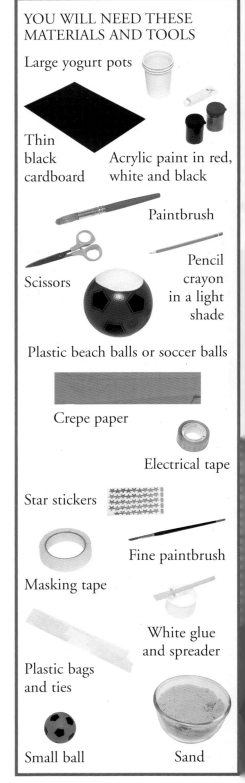

YOU WILL NEED THESE MATERIALS AND TOOLS

Large yogurt pots

Thin black cardboard

Acrylic paint in red, white and black

Paintbrush

Scissors

Pencil crayon in a light shade

Plastic beach balls or soccer balls

Crepe paper

Electrical tape

Star stickers

Fine paintbrush

Masking tape

White glue and spreader

Plastic bags and ties

Small ball

Sand

1 Paint the sides of the yogurt pots white. Leave to dry.

2 Draw a fun black moustache on black cardboard with a light pencil crayon and cut it out.

3 Paint a white circle onto your ball and leave it to dry. It is easier if you balance it on a yogurt pot or mug so that it doesn't roll around.

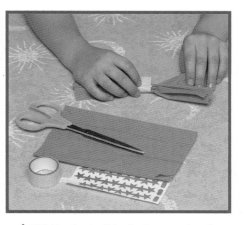

4 While the ball is drying, make the bow tie. Cut crepe paper so that it measures 15 x 10cm/6 x 4in. Fold it several times. Tie the middle with a piece of tape and stick on some stars.

5 Paint a face onto the ball using a fine brush and black and red acrylic paints.

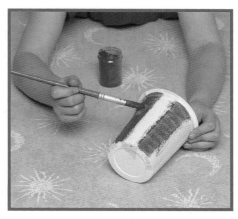

6 Once the paint on the yogurt pots is dry, stick strips of masking tape on them, leaving 2cm/1in gaps. Paint the gaps with red acrylic paint and leave to dry.

7 Stick the moustache and bow tie onto the ball. Peel the masking tape off the yogurt pots.

8 Fill a plastic bag with sand and twist a tie around the top. Place it in the pot and put the ball on top.

Apple Bobbing

This game is traditionally enjoyed at Halloween, but it is great to play at parties throughout the year. You have to get the apples out of the bowl without using your hands, as Moriam and Patrice are trying to do! It's a lot of fun, but you can get very wet, so wear something to protect your clothes.

A plastic apron would be perfect. It's also a good idea to put your bowl on a table in the kitchen. Decorate the bowl to suit your theme. Happy bobbing!

Finger paint
You can buy paint specially for finger painting, but acrylic paint is also fine. Have a cloth handy for cleaning up, as it can get very messy!

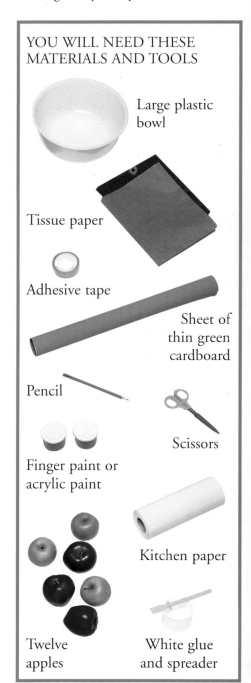

YOU WILL NEED THESE MATERIALS AND TOOLS

Large plastic bowl

Tissue paper

Adhesive tape

Sheet of thin green cardboard

Pencil

Finger paint or acrylic paint

Scissors

Kitchen paper

Twelve apples

White glue and spreader

1 To decorate the bowl, stick a folded wad of tissue paper just under the edge of the bowl with adhesive tape. Then gather the paper to fit around the bottom and tape it down. Do this with three more wads of tissue paper.

2 Draw an apple shape onto the thin green cardboard. Remember to use a pencil that will show up on green.

3 Cut the apple shape out, then draw around it to make three more apples. Cut them out, too.

4 Finger-paint the apples with red dots. Keep some kitchen paper to hand to wipe your fingers on, and wash your hands when you have finished.

5 Stick each apple onto the tissue paper with glue. Leave to dry.

6 Put the bowl on a waterproof table or floor and ask a grown-up to fill the bowl with water and all the apples.

Easter Egg Hunt

An Easter party is the perfect excuse for an egg hunt. Hide your decorated eggs around the house or the garden for all your friends to find. Clive is turning eggs into Easter rabbits. Count up your guests and then decorate the same number of eggs. Remember to make one for yourself, too! Some people blow the egg out of the shell, but it is easier to hard boil them – as long as you don't keep them too long.

YOU WILL NEED THESE MATERIALS AND TOOLS

One egg for each guest at your party

Saucepan and water

Egg carton   Ruler

Acrylic paint   Paintbrush

Thin cardboard in the shade of your choice

Crepe paper   Scissors

White glue and brush

Thick white paper   Pencil

Felt-tipped pen   Raffia

40

1 Ask a grown-up to put the eggs into cold water. Bring the water to the boil, and then boil the eggs for 10 minutes. Rinse the eggs in cold water to cool them. Then leave them to dry, propped up in the egg carton.

2 Once the eggs have dried, paint an oval shape on one side of them for the rabbit face. Leave the paint to dry.

3 Cut out rabbit ears from the cardboard, 6cm/2½in long and 3cm/1in at the widest point. Cut smaller pieces of crepe paper and stick them onto the ears with glue.

4 Draw the teeth on thick white paper – they should be 1.5cm/¾in by 1cm/½in. Cut them out.

5 Cut six raffia whiskers for each egg. They should be 5cm/2in long.

6 Stick the ears, whiskers and teeth onto the eggs with glue. To stick the ears on, fold a little part of the cardboard under, and stick that onto the egg. Leave to dry in the egg carton.

7 Draw on the eyes and nose in felt-tipped pen, to make a cheerful Easter bunny.

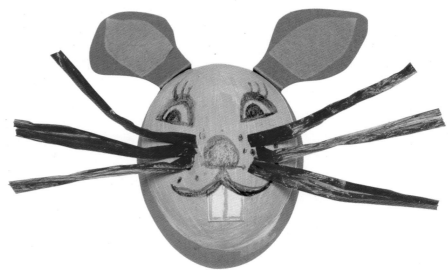

Marzipan Dinosaur Cake

Marzipan is the delicious almond decoration you find on the top of birthday cakes. You can buy marzipan from any supermarket and it's easy to liven it up with food dye. Decorate a ready-made cake for yourself or for someone in your family or a friend. Before you roll the marzipan, wash your hands.

YOU WILL NEED THESE MATERIALS AND TOOLS

Cake plate

Kitchen foil

Adhesive tape

Marzipan

Food dye in yellow, blue and green

Pencil

Paper plate

Scissors

Tracing paper

Cutting board

Rolling pin

Knife

Icing (confectioner's) sugar

Candle holders

Cake candles

1 Cover the plate with foil and use a little adhesive tape on the back to hold the foil in place.

2 Add food dye to the marzipan, only a couple of drops at a time. Knead it in thoroughly.

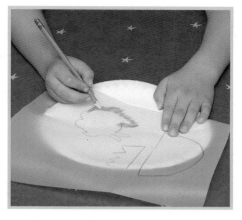

3 Trace the dinosaur template and transfer it onto the paper plate, using a soft pencil.

4 Cut out the dinosaur and the other shapes.

5 Roll out the marzipan to about 6mm/¼in thick. Sprinkle a little icing sugar onto the rolling pin and surface to stop the marzipan sticking.

6 Ask a grown-up to cut out the marzipan with a knife, using your paper-plate cut-outs as a guide.

7 Put the cake onto the plate covered in foil and carefully lay the marzipan on the cake. You can help the shapes stay in place by dabbing a bit of water underneath.

8 Push the candles into the holders, then decorate the cake with them. Light the candles and it's time to sing "Happy Birthday"!

Funny Face Cupcakes

These are cakes you can either decorate before your guests arrive, or make into a game at the party. Lay out all the materials and see which guest can make the silliest face or the most imaginative object out of the cakes. Iza and Gaby have made funny faces with mad hair.

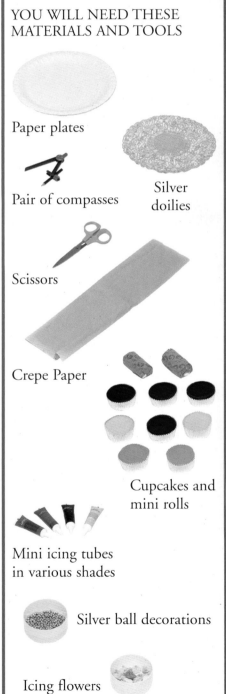

YOU WILL NEED THESE MATERIALS AND TOOLS

Paper plates

Pair of compasses

Silver doilies

Scissors

Crepe Paper

Cupcakes and mini rolls

Mini icing tubes in various shades

Silver ball decorations

Icing flowers

44

1 Put a silver doily on a paper plate. Using compasses, draw a slightly smaller circle on crepe paper and cut it out. Place it on top of the doily.

2 Place a cupcake and a mini roll on the plate. These will make the head and body.

3 Pipe on the mouth, eyes and nose, using different shades of icing. Take care to squeeze the mini icing tubes gently.

4 Put silver balls on the eyes to make them sparkle.

5 To make the jacket, ice on stripes and buttons. Add icing flower decorations and silver balls.

6 Add some curly hair with a different shade of icing.

7 Add arms, hands and a skirt by piping icing straight onto the crepe paper. Add some icing flowers for the feet – and now your work of art is ready to eat!

"Seven Today" Sandwiches

Patrice loves cheese sandwiches, but she wanted to make them a bit special for her party. As she is celebrating her seventh birthday she has made some special snacks in the shape of her new age. She has split the number seven sandwich into two so that it is easy to eat, bite by bite! The cress and radishes are not only healthy and decorative, but also delicious. Use parsley if you cannot get cress.

Clean cook alert

Don't forget to wash your hands before you start. And be careful when you're using a knife.

YOU WILL NEED THESE MATERIALS AND TOOLS

Paper napkins

Brown bread

Cress

Radishes

Large plate

Knife

Cheese

Cutting board